Listen
To the
Angels

by

John W. Eubank

King James Study Bible, Thomas Nelson Publishers 135BG, Center Column References and Notes are copyright 1998 by Thomas Nelson, Inc., (The King James Study Bible, previously published as the Liberty Annotated Study Bible, King James Version, Copyright 1988 by Liberty University).

Copyright © 2006   John W. Eubank

All rights reserved. No part of this publication may be reproduced, stored in a retrieval system, or transmitted in any form or by any means, electronic, mechanical, photocopying, recording, or otherwise, without the prior written permission of the publisher.

ISBN: 1-933899-28-X

Published by:
Holy Fire Publishing
531 Constitution Blvd., Martinsburg, WV 25405
www.ChristianPublish.com

Cover Design: Jay Cookingham

Printed in the United States of America and the United Kingdom

Dedication

I am dedicating this book to my three children because they helped me to get this book together, trusting that it will inspire them and others to do greater things for the Lord.

Quotes About Author (from 2 of his children):

"Dad was an inspiration to all his three children as well as anyone who knew him. He was a quiet and unassuming man who was an avid Bible student and who loved his Lord and the word of God."
 - Johnny Eubank

"My dad loved the Lord more than anyone I know. Although he rarely said "I love you", we all knew deep down how much he loved us. My dad taught me more about the Bible and our guardian angels in the last five years than anyone else in all my life. He has been my mentor and all of his explaining of the scriptures made me finally aware that, Yes, I am saved."
- Treva Seay

Quotes About the Book:

"I was absolutely astounded to learn of the different roles that the angels played in Biblical times, as well as in the present and in the future, and that they are present in our lives at all times."
-Debbie Johnson

"*Listen to the Angels* provides a unique glimpse into the role of angels in our everyday lives. Mr. Eubank provides personal explanations without forcing opinions or beliefs on the reader."
- Amanda Van Patten

"*Listen to the Angels* has opened my eyes to the stark realities of the book of Revelation and the second coming of Christ that most of us take for granted. It's time we all think seriously about listening to the angels."
- Rob Johnson, Jr.

"This book has changed our thoughts about angels."
- Sloan Kuykendall

Just as Jesus Christ is bright like the sun, we must be like the moon, and reflect his sunshine and glory in the darkest of hours.

-Anonymous

Topics Covered in this Book

Angels do not have wings

Good angels

Bad angels

Angels are messengers

Angels smile when one repents

Angels guard and protect

Angels eat and drink

Angels give warnings

Angels know what you are doing

Angels visit

Angels are supernatural

Angels are real

Angels talk

Angels escort you home

Angels that sinned

Listen to the Angels

In order to listen to the angels, we must go to the Hebrew and Greek dictionaries to learn just what an angel is. In the Strong's Concordance (page 4397), we find the word "mal'ak", from an unused root word meaning to dispatch as a messenger of God; also a prophet, priest or teacher, and ambassador. In Greek, it could be a minister.

Many people think of angels as being something like a ghost flying around with a big pair of white wings. This is far from the truth, because angels do not have wings and they are around or near us at all times. If we would stop long enough to realize it, then we could live in a peaceful world. Your personal angel looking down from heaven has its eyes on you and knows exactly what you are doing and thinking.

Here I will quote Matthew 18:10, "Take heed that ye despise not one of these little ones, which is God's children; for I say unto you that in heaven their angels do always behold the face of our Father which is in heaven."

Angels are as an appearance of God in human form. When angels appeared to the prophets and others in the Old Testament, they did not know whether they were angels or just another man, only at certain times. I say this because many times we entertain angels without even knowing it.

When God said, "let us make man in our own image", that is what he meant and that is what he did, no man has a big pair of wings to fly around with. When God said this, he was talking to his heavenly host of angels. Many ask the question as to who God was talking to; well here you have the answer.

"Listen to the Angels"

When Christ was here, he was in the exact image of God the Father and he did not have wings. Christ, being in the flesh, tells us that no man has wings, and this tells us that when we hear a real prophet (which we do not have today) or a real priest, teacher, or minister, then we are listening to angels without being aware of it. When angels speak to you and you know that they are real, then there should be some kind of action on your part.

I will use some examples from scripture to point this out and you should listen. I will start with Abraham in Genesis 22:10, where he stretched forth his hand and took the knife to slay his son.

Verse 11: "And the angel of the Lord called unto him out of heaven, and said, Abraham, Abraham: and he said, Here am I." Verse 15: "And the angel of the Lord called unto Abraham out of heaven the second time"; verse 16 - "And said, By myself have I sworn, saith the Lord, for because thou hath done this thing, and hast not withheld thy son, thine only son (verse 17) that in blessing I will bless

"Listen to the Angels"

thee, and in multiplying I will multiply thy seed as the stars of heaven, and the sand which is upon the sea shores, and thy seed shall possess the gate of his enemies (verse 18) and in thy seed shall all the nations of the earth be blessed; because thou hast obeyed my voice". We can see here that when the angel of the Lord spoke to Abraham, he listened and the blessings came.

Exodus 3:2 says, "And the angel of the Lord appeared unto him in a flame of fire out of the midst of a bush, and he looked, and behold, the bush burned with fire, and the bush was not consumed." Verse 4 – "And when the Lord saw that he turned aside to see, God called unto him out of the midst of the bush, and said, Moses, Moses, and he said, Here am I."

We can hear people today asking the question that if the bush was on fire, why was it not consumed? Well, if God called to Moses out of the midst of the bush, then we know that God did not

"Listen to the Angels"

burn up and it was his "shekinah" glory that encircled the bush, and Moses thought that it was burning.

We should know the rest of the message is that God used Moses to lead his people out of bondage in Egypt because he listened to the angel. Moses argued a little with God and said that he could not speak well and was not the right one for the job, but God had already spoken to him and said, "You are the one", and Moses listened and obeyed. In doing so, it made him a type of a savior.

Angels are mentioned 297 times in the scripture and it would take a volume of books to spell out all of their doings, so I will mention some of their visitations to earthly people and to say that these people listened. He spoke to Hagar, to Abraham, to Lot, to Balaam, to the Israelites, to Gideon, to Manoah's wife, to David, to Elijah, and to Daniel. He also spoke to Nebuchadnezzar, to Jesus, to Joseph, to Mary Magdalene, to Zacharias, to the Virgin Mary. Also, he spoke to the shepherds, to Peter and others, to Philip, to Cornelius, and to Paul.

"Listen to the Angels"

I mention them because they were chosen to help carry out God's plan. We were also chosen for the same reason, but we do not have angels visiting us from heaven as of times past. We do have God's word, the Bible, and he expects us to read, heed, listen and act. If we cannot connect with his word, then we can listen to the ones who have the truth and can help direct the way. You might ask the question as to how do I know who to listen to? Well, if someone comes to you and they prove that they understand the truth about God's word, his plan for mankind and his plan for redeeming them of their sin, then we can listen to them.

Then there is also this still, small voice that speaks to us, telling us what is wrong and what is right. This is a natural built-in gift from God, but we have to recognize it and put it to use. We might call this our guardian angel, but we must listen.

To make it a little simpler to understand the voice, I will use this illustration. Suppose that you are walking through your yard and came up on a big rattlesnake. What is the first thing that comes to your mind, as it is lying there with its rattlers straight up and rattling a warning tune, telling you not to come any closer. I can bet that you would not lose any time getting out of its way. On the other hand, if you went any closer, you know that you are going to get bitten, and if there is not a quick fix, then you could very well die.

It is the same way with sin. You know better than to touch says the still, small voice; but if you do, you are going to die (because sin is death). Unless you repent and back off like you would with the snake, you are going to die. I say this because if you have Christ in you, then you can have power over all of your enemies, including the snake, the devil and anything that is evil. I will remind you that you have to listen when the voice speaks.

I would like to mention the only two angels in the scripture that are named, Gabriel and Michael. There is much to be said about them and I will give you just part of their visitations with earthly men.

"Listen to the Angels"

Gabriel's visitation to Zacharias: Zacharias and his wife are described as "righteous before God, walking in all the commandments and ordinances of the Lord blameless" (Luke 1:6). On one occasion when he was serving in the temple, Zacharias was burning incense and was confronted by the angel Gabriel, who announced to him that Elizabeth would have a son. Since Elizabeth was barren and well past the normal age of child-bearing, Zacharias could hardly believe the words of the angel and for his skepticism was struck dumb. At the birth of the child, Zacharias complied with the instructions of the angel and insisted that the child be named John. When this was agreed upon, Zacharias recovered his speech.

You can see that if and when an angel speaks to you, there is not room for argument. If Zacharias had kept his cool and listened, then he would not have been stricken dumb and John the Baptist would have arrived anyway. Thanks be to God that John

"Listen to the Angels"

was chosen to pave the way for the coming of Jesus Christ, the savior of the world.

Michael, the other angel, is one that should be listened to even today, because if we can understand the first verse in Daniel 12:1, concerning the time of the end, we will open our ears and heed. Daniel 12:1 reads as follows, "And at that time shall Michael stand up, the great prince which standeth for thy people, and there shall be a time of trouble such as never was since there was a nation even to that same time; and at that time thy people shall be delivered, everyone that shall be found written in the book."

God is using Michael as a special angel to help bring this world age to its end. We can read in Revelation 12:7-12 where it is Michael who leads the angelic host against the dragon, Satan, and his forces, casting them out of heaven. And guess what, it is intended for them to land on this earth and woe to its inhabitants.

Michael is pictured as possessing a warlike character. In the book of Daniel, he appears as a

"Listen to the Angels"

heavenly champion of the people of Israel. Jude refers to him as having opposed the devil in contest over the bones of Moses. You may ask the question as to why Michael opposed the devil over the bones of Moses. We all should know that Moses was the law giver, and when the people obeyed the law, then they were blessed. On the other hand, when they disobeyed the law they were cursed, and the devil did not like it when the law was obeyed because it kept him from having his way with them.

The devil hated Moses and wanted to destroy his bones. It is not written that Moses was buried when he died, so what happened to him? My best guess is that God took him as he did Elijah. The reason I say this is because when Jesus was transfigured, Elijah and Moses were there with him and they actually talked with the disciples. I can imagine that the devil is going to want his bones, but did you know he won't get them because Jesus is going to crush Satan and all that he stands for. You can read all about it in the book of Revelation.

"Listen to the Angels"

I will mention another one who refused to listen to God or the angel of the Lord, that one being Balaam. Most Bible students should be familiar with him, but there are many who don't know one thing about him. I will try to relate the story to you and just maybe you will understand the importance of listening to angels. Most scripture portray him as an opponent of Israel, who would have crushed Israel had not a sovereign God intervened. He was also a man who preferred money for serving God. In II Peter 2:1-15, he is in the context of false prophets, which have forsaken the right way and are gone astray.

I will use some scripture from Numbers 22, beginning with verse 21, to show you just how bad Balaam went astray and how he would not listen to what God told him not to do. Verse 21 – "And Balaam rose up in the morning, and saddled his ass, and went with the princes of Moab." Verse 22 – "And God's anger was kindled because he went: and the angel of the Lord stood in the way for an adversary against him. Now he was riding upon his ass, and his two servants were with him". Verse 23 – "And the ass saw the angel of the Lord standing in the way, and his sword drawn in his hand: and the ass turned aside out of the way, and went into the field: and Balaam smote the ass, to turn her into the way." Verse 24 – "But the angel of the Lord stood in a path of the vineyards, a wall being on this side, and a wall on that side." Verse 25 – "And when the ass saw the angel of the Lord, she thrust herself unto the wall, and crushed Balaam's foot against the wall: and he smote her again". Verse 26 – "And the angel of the Lord went further, and stood in a narrow place, where there was no where to turn either to the right hand or to the left." Verse 27 – "And when the ass saw the angel of the Lord, she fell down under Balaam: and Balaam's anger was kindled, and he smote the ass with a staff." Verse 28 – "And the Lord opened the mouth of the ass, and she said unto Balaam, What have I done unto thee, that thou hast smitten me these three times?". Verse 29 – "And

"Listen to the Angels"

Balaam said unto the ass, Because thou hast mocked me: I would there were a sword in mine hand, for now would I kill thee". Verse 30 – "And the ass said unto Balaam, Am not I thine ass, upon which thou hast ridden ever since I was thine unto this day? Was I ever won't to do so unto thee? And he said, Nay". Verse 31 – "Then the Lord opened the eyes of Balaam, and he saw the angel of the Lord standing in the way, and his sword drawn in his hand: and he bowed down his head, and fell flat on his face." Verse 32 – "And the angel of the Lord said unto him, Wherefore hast thou smitten thine ass these three times? Behold, I went out to withstand thee, because thy way is perverse before me: (verse 33) and the ass saw me, and turned from me these three times, unless she had turned from me, surely I also would have slain thee, and saved her alive". Verse 34 – "And Balaam said unto the angel of the Lord, I have sinned; for I knew not that thou stoodest in the way against me: now therefore, if it displease thee, I will get me back again". Verse 35 – "And the angel of the Lord said unto Balaam, Go with the men: but only the word that I shall speak unto thee, that thou shall speak". So Balaam went with the princes of Balak.

The reason that I chose chapter 22 of Numbers is because I wanted you to see that if you do not listen to angels, then God has other ways to get your attention, like causing Balaam's ass to speak to him before he could get God's message. You can see that God uses whomever or whatever he chooses to get you to listen to him, even if it is a so called dumb ass. I would like to point out that angels are in special form, in which God manifested himself to man, and hence Christ's visible form before the incarnation.

We ordinarily understand angels as a race of spiritual beings of a nature exalted far above that of man, whose office is to do God's service in heaven, and by his appointment to "succor and defend men on earth". There are many passages in which the expression "angel of God" is used for a manifestation of God himself, as in Genesis 22:11-12 and Exodus 3:2-14.

"Listen to the Angels"

It is also observed that side by side with these expressions, we read of God's being manifested in the form of man – as to Abraham at Mamre (Genesis 18:1-22), also as in Genesis 19:1 to Jacob. Genesis 32 verse 30 states that Jacob saw God "face to face". Another place we find this same kind of appearance is in Joshua 5:13-15.

In the highest application of the word "angel", we find the phrase used of any messenger of God, such as prophets, priests and the rulers of the Christian churches in Revelation 1:20. The nature of angels is termed "spirits" as in Hebrews 1:14, but it is not asserted that the angelic nature is incorporeal. The angels are revealed to us as beings such as man might be, and will be when the power of sin and death are removed. Therefore "being made like him", their numbers are large and have great strength. Their activity is marvelous, their appearance varies according to circumstances, but they can be brilliant and dazzling (Matthew 28:2-7 and Revelation: 10:1-2).

"Listen to the Angels"

We know little about the nature of "fallen angels", or the circumstances and motive of the temptation by which they fell. All that is certain is that they "left their first estate", and that they are now "angels of the devil". On the other hand, the title specially assigned to the angels of God – that of the "holy ones", is precisely the one which is given to those men who are renewed in Christ's image (Hebrews 2:10, 5:9 and 12:23).

When I mention the good and bad angels, you should be very careful which ones to listen to. Of angels offices in heaven we have only a glimpse of their doings, but the scriptures tell us of a never ending adoration. They are represented as being, in the broadest sense, agents of God's providence, both natural and supernatural, to the body and soul. In other words, they are Christ's ministers of grace now, as they shall be of judgment hereafter.

There are degrees of the angelic nature, both fallen and unfallen, and special titles and agencies belonging to each. This is clearly declared by Paul in

"Listen to the Angels"

Ephesians 1:21 and Romans 8:38, but what their general nature is, we can only speculate.

Here I will try to explain the nature of one angel that we all should be familiar with and should never listen to. There are many around the world that do listen to him and place their only soul in his hands. That angel is none other than Satan. Many ask the question that if Satan is an angel and became the devil, why did God create such a being? God did not expect him to turn out to be the devil, he made the choice himself and I will use some scripture to point this out to you.

First of all, he fell through pride, and this is what gets so many today in trouble. I Timothy 3:6 states that "a novice, lest being lifted up with pride he fall into the condemnation of the devil." Verse 7 – "moreover he must have a good report of them which are without; lest he fall into reproach and the snare of the devil."

You and I have the same choice today to either follow Satan or the real angels. When Satan, the devil, fell from his place as an angel, he also took one third of God's children with him, by listening to his deceiving words and ways. Are you listening to him by his deceiving ways? If so, it is time to wake up and find out all you can about him and what he stands for. Just maybe you will not be caught in his snares.

To point out more that Satan was a perfect angel, I will use the scripture from the book of Ezekiel, Chapter 28, beginning with verse 6 – "Therefore thus saith the Lord God; Because thou has set thine heart as the heart of God"; verse 7 – "Behold, therefore I will bring strangers upon thee, the terrible of the nations: and they shall draw their swords against the beauty of thy wisdom, and they shall defile thy brightness" (meaning splendor). Verse 8 – "They shall bring thee down to the pit, and thou shalt die the deaths of them that are slain in the midst of the seas". Verse 10 – "Thou shalt die the deaths of the uncircumcised by the hands of strangers; for I have spoken it saith the Lord God". Verse 12 – "Thus saith the Lord God; Thou sealest up the sum, full of wisdom, and perfect in beauty"; verse 13 – "Thou hast been in Eden, the garden of God; and every precious stone was thy covering, the sardius, topaz, and the diamond, the beryl, the onyx, and the jasper, the sapphire, the emerald, and the carbuncle and gold: the workmanship of thy tabrets and of thy pipes was prepared in thee in the day that thou wast created". Verse 14 – "Thou are the anointed cherub that covereth; and I have set thee so; thou was upon the holy mountain of God; thou hast walked up and down in the midst of the stones of fire". Verse 15 – "Thou was perfect in thy ways from the day that thou was created, till iniquity was found in thee". Verse 16 – "By the multitude of thy merchandise they have filled the midst of thee with violence, and thou hast sinned – therefore, I will cast thee as profane out of the mountain of God; and I will destroy thee, O covering cherub, from the midst of the stones of fire". Verse 17 – "Thine heart was lifted up because of thy beauty, thou hast corrupted thy wisdom by reason of thy brightness: I will cast thee to the ground, I will lay thee before kings, that they may behold thee" (see Revelation 12). Verse 18 – "Thou hast defiled thy sanctuaries by the multitude of thine iniquities, by the iniquity of thy traffick; therefore I will bring forth a fire from the midst of thee, it shall devour thee, and I will bring thee to ashes upon the earth in the sight of all them that behold thee." Verse 19 – "All they that know thee among the people shall be astonished at thee: thou shalt be a terror, and never shalt thou be anymore".

Do you want to listen to an angel like this, which has gone so bad that he turned into the devil? I have said before that Satan took one third of the host with him when he fell. These are called the "fallen angels". We can find their doom in 2 Peter 2:4 and it says, "For God spared not the angels that sinned. But cast them down to hell and delivered them into chains of darkness, to be reserved unto judgment".

In Jude 6, we can see that "The angels who kept not their first estate but left their own habitation, he hath reserved in everlasting chains under darkness unto the judgment of the great day." These angels are the ones that will appear when Satan and his followers are thrown out of heaven to this earth (Revelation 12).

We can see from Matthew 24:37 that "As the days of Noah were, so shall also the coming of the son of man be". Verse 38 – "For as in the days that were before the flood they were eating and drinking, marrying and given in marriage, until the day that Noah entered into the ark". Verse 39 – "And knew not until the flood came, and took them all away; so shall also the coming of the Son of man be".

You may ask the question as to who were these that were marrying and given in marriage? These are the fallen angels that left their first estate and came down to the daughters of Adam, then intermixed to bring forth the ones that were so evil that God caused the flood to destroy them all. When these angels return in the book of Revelation, we are warned in 1 Corinthians 11:10, that women especially ought to have power on their heads because of the angels. This power means having the authority to defeat them with God's word in their mind. The only way that women and men can have this power is to get into God's word and try to understand just how serious it is to listen to these angels because they are Satan's angels.

I would like to mention two other angels that I cannot say much about, except that they were special angels that looked after God's throne, these two angels are Cherubim and Seraphim. They may have had wings as some artists portray and I think that the reason that Ezekiel and John in Revelation thought that they were some kind of beast was because they had never seen anything like them before. The reason that they thought that they were some kind of beast is the way they are described in Ezekiel 10, which says their basic form was that of a winged sphinx or winged lion with a human head. Surely this would confuse anyone.

"Listen to the Angels"

We can see from Genesis 3:24 where "God drove the man out of the Garden of Eden and placed Cherubim east of the garden with a flaming sword which turned every way, to keep the way of the tree of life." You can bet your life that if anyone or anything did not listen to these Cherubim, they would be slaughtered. You can read much about the Cherubim and Seraphim throughout the scripture, and it would be good for you to search it out.

I would like to say more about the nature of good angels. First, they exercise authority, they can inspire terror, can afford protection, can utter predictions, permit oblations, are identified with God, are superhuman, can appear as men, can wear human apparel, and some men are compared with angels.

The office of angels is to wait on God, announce God's laws, convey God's messages, protect God's people and inflict divine penalties. They are ministering spirits, guardians of cities and nations; they share in the councils of God, sound the apocalyptic trumpets and gather the elect to judgment. Do you listen to their messages?

Here is a summary of what the writer of Hebrews has to say about the angels: Angels are created, spiritual beings who are servants of God. The word angel means "messenger" as stated earlier. They also have power to become visible in human form. They are beings, possessing intellect, emotion, and will.

The word "angel" is always used in the masculine gender, although sex in the human sense is never ascribed to them. They have great power (II Kings 19:35), but are not omnipotent. They have extensive wisdom (2 Samuel 14:20), their number is great (Hebrews 12:22), but not limitless. Illustration: man is made "a little lower than the angels" (Hebrews 2:7) although the same writer reminds us that Christ is greater than the angels. There are a number of benefits derived from understanding the ministry of angels.

"Listen to the Angels"

When we realize that they constantly observe our Christian lives (I Corinthians 4:9, 11:10 & Ephesians 3:10) we will improve our conduct. When we understand how they protect us, we will appreciate God's care for us. When we consider their tremendous strength and ability, we will be encouraged.

Finally, their example of unceasing service ought to motivate us to more consistent service for God. First reference (Genesis 1:1 – "heaven" is plural in Hebrew, meaning God created the whole, with its innumerable separate parts, including angels; primary reference Hebrews 1:4 and 12:22). The main point in chapters one and two of Hebrews is that Christ is superior to the angels because of the work that he has accomplished.

In Hebrews 1 verses 4-14, the writer proves Christ's superiority by citing seven Old Testament passages. It was necessary that he prove to his readers Christ's superiority over the angels, for in the first-century world, pagan and Christian alike accorded great significance and power to angels. Some had taught that Christ himself was an angel, and for that reason, able to perform miracles. There is evidence from scripture in Colossians 2:18 that some even worshipped angels.

Angels were also involved in the giving of the Mosaic Law (Col. 2:2, Acts 7:53, Gal. 3:19) thus, if the author wishes to prove the overall superiority of Christ, he must prove that Christ is superior to the angels.

Jesus' superiority to the angels is presented in a sevenfold manner (from Hebrews Chapter 1).

1. Being the son, he has a better name than they (vs.4,5);

2. He is worshipped (vs. 6); and

3. Served by the angels (vs. 7);

4. Jesus is God (vs. 8)

5. He created the angels (vs. 10)

6. Is from everlasting to everlasting (vs. 11-12)

7. Sits at God's right hand (Vs. 13) and the dignity of the Son is the dignity of God, but the

dignity of the angels is that of mere servants (vs. 14). The book of Hebrews contains five warning passages, these passages contain much exhortation but also some explicit warnings – a danger sign.

The first passage warns: do not neglect Christ's message. Since God has no greater messenger than his Son, he has no more important message than the gospel which the Son has given. If the law given through the angels was steadfast, producing sure judgment, how shall we escape if we ignore the sure message of the son? This message was proclaimed by Christ to his apostles and then by the apostles to the author of Hebrews. I trust that you are getting the message that Christ and his angels are conveying to you, and pay special attention to their warnings. These are warnings that you must listen to if you ever expect to be one of God's heirs.

The relation of angels to the believer is that of "ministering spirits, sent forth to minister for them who shall be heirs of salvation" (Hebrews 1:14), and this ministry has reference largely to the physical

"Listen to the Angels"

safety and wellbeing of believers (I Kings 19:5, Psalms 34:7 & 91:11, Daniel 6:22, Matthew 2:13-19 & 4:11, Luke 22:43, and Acts 5:19 & 12:7-10). From Hebrews 1:14, Matthew 18:10 and Psalms 91:11, it would seem that this care for the heirs of salvation begins in infancy and continues through life.

The angels observe us (I Corinthians 4:9, Ephesians 3:10, and Ecclesiastes 5:6), a fact which should influence conduct. They receive departing spirits (Luke 16:22). Man is made a "little lower than the angels", and in incarnation, Christ took ("for a little time") this lower place (Psalms 8:4-5, Hebrews 2:6-9), that he might lift the believer into his own sphere above angels (Hebrews 2: 9-10). The angels are to accompany Christ in his second advent (Matthew 25:31), to them will be committed the preparation of the judgment of nations.

Since the angels observe us, we should be careful how we participate in the things of this world. Listen to their voice so that when we stand before the judgment to receive our rewards, we won't be among the goats on God's left hand to receive the punishment that Satan and his angels will receive, which will be eternal death. Eternal death is the death of the soul to be no more.

The ministration of holy angels, as presented in the scriptures, is a truth most comforting and precious to every follower of Christ. On the other hand, the fallen angels are to be very discomforting because they are Satan's angels. Satan's angels are out to deceive God's elect if they do not have Christ and his word fixed in their minds to defeat them. There are two classes of fallen angels mentioned in scripture. One being the ones that left their first estate and left their own habitation, and are "chained in darkness" awaiting judgment (II Peter 2:4, Jude 6, I Corinthians 6:3, John 5:22). Then the other class of fallen angels are those who have Satan as their leader (Genesis 3:1, Revelation 20:10), and may be identical to the devils (demons) of Matthew 7:22. For Satan and his angels, everlasting death is prepared. These

"Listen to the Angels"

are two classes of angels that you surely do not want to listen to.

We should acquaint ourselves with God by listening to the angels because they hear and record every prayer that is earnest and sincere. (In fact, Jacob even wrestled with the angel of God until his prayer was answered.) In doing so, we would not be seduced into sin and travel a path expecting God's blessings. Jacob was in trouble and fleeing from his brother, Esau, who was going to kill him. When he wrestled with the angel, he would not let him loose until he received the blessing that he would be safe. I say this so you can see that you have to be serious and believe to receive a blessing from God.

One who sees their every weakness, who is acquainted with every trial, and is above all earthly powers will have angels come to them in lovely places, bringing light and peace from heaven, as when Paul and Silas prayed and sang praises at midnight in the Philippians dungeon. We have to know as they did, that God is on our side as long as we have faith in him. Trust and believe in him and his messengers, the angels, and He will hear us.

If men could see with heavenly vision, they would see companies of angels that have much strength stationed around those who have kept the word of Christ. With compassion and tenderness, angels have witnessed their distress and have heard their prayers. They are awaiting the word of their master to get them out of their peril. However, they must wait a little longer, for God is not ready to bring them home. The heavenly sentinels, faithful to their trust, continue their watch. None can pass these mighty guardians stationed about every faithful soul.

In all ages, God has wrought through holy angels for the safety and deliverance of his people. Angels have taken an active part in the affairs of men. They have appeared clothed in garments that shone like lightning. They have come as men, in the way of wayfarers. Angels have appeared in human form to men of God. They have rested, as if weary, under the oaks. They have accepted the welcome of human homes. They have acted as guides to weary travelers, of course, when they listened and took their advice.

They have, with their own hands, kindled the fires of the alter. They have opened prison doors and set free the servants of the Lord. Clothed with the garments of heaven, they came to roll away the stone from the Savior's tomb. In the form of men, angels have been in the assemblies of the righteous. They also visit the assemblies of the wicked, as they went to Sodom to take record of their deeds to determine whether they had passed the boundary of God's warning.

In the councils of rulers, angels have been spokesmen. Human eyes have looked upon them, human ears have listened to their appeals and human lips have opposed their suggestions and ridiculed their counsel. Human hands have met them with insult and abuse. In the court of justice and council halls, these heavenly messengers have shown an acquaintance with human history. They have proven themselves better able to plead the cause of the oppressed better than the most able defenders.

They have defeated and stopped many evils that would have retarded the work of God, and would have caused great suffering to his people. In the hour of distress, the angel of the Lord was around about them that reverenced him (ref. Psalms 34:7).

To show further how angels help in the hour of distress, you can see from Daniel 6:22, where Daniel said, "My God hath sent his angel, and hath shut the lions' mouth that they have not hurt me: forasmuch as before him innocence was found in me; and also before thee, O king, I have done no hurt". We can see once again how angels visit earthly men.

Again in Daniel 3:24, "Then Nebuchadnezzar, the king, was astonished and rose up in hosts, and spake, and said unto his counselors, Did not we cast three men bound into the midst of the fire? They answered and said unto the king, True O king". Verse 25 - "He answered and said, Lo, I see four men loose, walking in the midst of the fire, and they have no hurt: and the form of the fourth is like the son of

God". Verse 28 - "Then the king spake and said, Blessed be the God of Shadrach, Meshach, and Abednego, who hath sent his angel, and delivered his servants that trusted in him". Since we are speaking of Daniel, I will direct you to where he saw the vision of the glory of God. In Daniel 10:5, it says "Then I lifted up mine eyes and looked, and behold a certain man clothed in linen, who's loins were girded with fine gold and Uphaz". Verse 6 - "His body also was like the beryl, and his face as the appearance of lightning, and his eyes as lamps of fire, and his arms and his feet like in color to polished brass, and the voice of his words like the voice of a multitude."

Revelation 1:13 refers to the vision of John while on the Isle of Patmos, like the vision of Daniel. He saw in Revelation 1:13 "in the midst of the seven candlesticks one like unto the Son of man, clothed with a garment down to the foot, and girt about the paps with a golden girdle". Verse 14- "His head and hair were white like wool, as white as snow: and his eyes were as a flame of fire". Verse 15 - "And his feet

"Listen to the Angels"

like unto fine brass, as if they had burned in a furnace; and his voice as the sound of many waters". Verse 16 - "And he had in his right hand seven stars: and out of his mouth went a sharp two-edged sword: and his countenance was as the sun shineth in his strength". Verse 17 - "And when I saw him, I fell at his feet as dead. And he laid his right hand upon me, saying unto me, Fear not; I am the first and the last". Verse 18 - "I am he that liveth, and was dead and behold, I am alive for evermore, Amen; and have the keys of hell and death". The great and shining one commanded to John in Verse 19- "Write the things which thou hast seen, and the things which are, and the things which all be hereafter."

Just in case you missed the seven stars in his right hand and do not know the meaning - verse 20 spells it out for you. Revelation verse 20 - "The mystery of the seven stars which thou sawest in my right hand, and the seven golden candlesticks. The seven stars are the angels of the seven churches: and the seven golden candlesticks which thou sawest are the seven churches" (refer to Revelation chapters 2 & 3).

You can see of the seven churches that Christ was pleased with only two of them by what they taught. If we know what these two churches taught and if we don't teach the same, then a lot of churches are going to be hurting when Christ checks them out again. We can see from Daniel's vision, along with John's vision, that they both were looking into the future, and had they not listened to God and the angels, we probably would not know what the future brings and would not know how to defeat Satan. These are two very important books of the Bible and we all should be digging into them.

To point out further how angels appear on earth and talk with people, in Matthew 28:2, it says "And behold there was a great earthquake: for the angel of the Lord descended from heaven, and came and rolled back the stone from the door, and sat upon it." Verse 3 - "His countenance was like lightning and his raiment white as snow " (we can see that his countenance was like the one we read about in Daniel). Verse 4 - "And for fear of him, the keepers did shake, and became as dead men, speechless". Verse 5 - "And the angel answered and said unto the women, Fear not ye; for I know that you seek Jesus, who was crucified". Verse 6 - "He is not here: for he is risen, as he said, come see the place where the Lord lay". Verse 7 - "And go quickly, and tell his disciples that he is risen from the dead: and behold, he goeth before you into Galilee; there shall ye see him: lo, I have told you". You can see from this that the angel had a lot to say to the women that were seeking Jesus. They listened and speedily went to tell the disciples.

In Luke 15:10 there is one very important thing about angels, for it says "Likewise, I say unto you, there is joy in the presence of the angels of God over one sinner that repenteth". Have you repented of all your sins so that the angels in heaven can rejoice? They are there waiting for you at anytime to hear you say, "Lord, I am a sinner and I repent. I pray for thy forgiveness".

"Listen to the Angels"

I would like to point out another place that shows just how real angels are. Let us take a look at Genesis 19:1, where two angels came to announce judgment on Sodom and Gomorrah: "And Lot seeing them rose up to meet them; and he bowed himself with his face toward the ground; and he said, (verse 2) Behold now, my Lord, turn in I pray you, into your servant's house and tarry all night, and wash your feet, and ye shall rise up early and go your ways, and they said, Nay; but we will abide in the street all night". Verse 3 - "And he pressed upon them greatly; and they turned in unto him, and entered into his house; and he made a feast, and did bake unleavened bread, and they did eat".

Read on through to verse 24, where the Lord rained upon Sodom and Gomorrah brimstone and fire from out of heaven. I wanted to point this out so you could see that the angels talked and listened while Lot spake to them, and they did eat as anyone else would eat. They acted and did what God sent them to do, and the two cities and the places round about went up in flames.

I will point out that angels are going to be used to announce judgment on this whole world. We can read all about it in the book of Revelation. In Matthew 25 we can see how Jesus answers the Sadducees by saying, "Now there was with us seven brethren: and the first, when he had married a wife, deceased, and, having no issue, left his wife to his brother". Verse 26 - "Likewise the second also, and the third, unto the seventh". Verse 27 - "And last of all, the woman died also". Now the Sadducees questioned in Verse 28 - "Therefore in the resurrection whose wife shall she be of the seven? For they all had her." They were trying to get Jesus to say that there was no resurrection. Jesus answered them by saying, "Ye do err, not knowing the scriptures, nor the power of God. For in the resurrection they neither marry, nor are given in marriage, but are as the angels of God in heaven". When the Sadducees listened to the answer that Jesus gave them, they were put to silence, but they

"Listen to the Angels"

continued to try to trick him by asking questions until they saw that they were beaten down.

In Romans 8: 38-39 we read, "For I am persuaded, that neither death, nor life, nor angels, nor principalities, nor powers, nor things present, nor things to come, nor height, nor depth, nor any other creature, shall be able to separate us from the love of God." Are you listening to these two scripture verses? You can see that nothing can separate us from God when we repent of our sins and put our trust in him.

In Luke 15:10 it says, "Likewise, I say unto you, there is joy in the presence of the angels of God over one sinner that repenteth". There are thousands out there that need to listen to this.

In Acts 8:39, we read of a eunuch of great authority. Acts 8 verse 26 states that "The angel of the Lord spake unto Philip, saying, Arise and go toward the south unto the way that goeth down from Jerusalem". On his way he met this eunuch who requested to be baptized when he had heard what the

"Listen to the Angels"

scriptures and Philip said to him, and by a pool of water by the way, he was baptized. By Philip listening to the angel , the eunuch was saved. Here again we can see that angels do appear to men and talk to them, and they act.

I would like to point out other scriptures in the Old Testament where angels visited men. In Genesis 18: 1-9, we read that, "Angels appeared unto Abraham as he sat in the tent door in the heat of the day. And he lifted up his eyes and looked, and lo, three men stood by him: and when he saw them, he ran to meet them from the tent door, and bowed himself toward the ground. And he said, My Lord, if now I have found favor in thy sight, pass not away, I pray thee, from thy servant. Let a little water, I pray you, be fetched, and wash your feet, and rest yourselves under the tree. And I will fetch a morsel of bread, and comfort ye your hearts; after that ye shall pass on: for therefore are ye come to your servant, and they said, So do, as thou hast said. And Abraham hastened into the tent unto Sarah, and said, make ready quickly three measures of fine meal, knead it, and make cakes upon the hearth. And Abraham ran unto the herd, and fetched a calf tender and good, and gave it unto a young man; and he hastened to dress it. And he took butter, and milk, and the calf which he had dressed, and set it before them; and he stood by them under the tree, and they did eat".

Genesis 18:16, "And the men rose up from thence, and looked toward Sodom: and Abraham went with them to bring them on their way". Verse 17 - "And the Lord said, Shall I hide from Abraham that thing which I do;" Verse 18 - "Seeing that Abraham shall surely become a great and mighty nation, and all the nations of the earth shall be blessed in him?" Verse 19 - "For I know him, that he will command his children and his household after him, and they shall keep the way of the Lord, to justice and judgment; that the Lord may bring upon Abraham that which he hast spoken of him". Verse 20 & 21 - "And the Lord said, Because the cry of Sodom and

"Listen to the Angels"

Gomorrah is great, and because their sin is very grievous; I will go down now, and see whether they have done altogether, according to the cry of it, which is come unto me; and if not I will know". Here is where Abraham pleads with God not to destroy the two cities if he could find at least ten righteous people there. Sadly, he could not and God sent two angels to announce their judgment.

Genesis 19:1 - "And there came two angels to Sodom at even; and Lot sat in the gate of Sodom: and Lot seeing (them) rose up to meet them; and he bowed himself with his face toward the ground;" Verse 2 - "And he said, Behold now, my Lords, turn in I pray you, into your servant's house, and tarry all night, and wash your feet, and ye shall rise up early, and go on your ways, and they said, Nay; but we will abide in the street all night". Verse 3 - "And he pressed upon them greatly: and they turned in unto him, and entered into his house; and he made them a feast, and did bake unleavened bread, and they did eat".

"Listen to the Angels"

I point these verses out so we can see and know that angels are real. They knew Abraham and Lot, and talked with them and they did eat, just as anyone else, and they did not have wings to fly around with. Going to verse 12, "And the men (angels) said unto Lot, Hast thou here besides? Son-in-law, and thy sons, and thy daughters, and whatsoever thou hast in the city, bring them out of this place:" Verse 13 - "For I will destroy this place, because the cry of them is waxen great before the face of the Lord; and the Lord hast sent us to destroy it".

Here you can see that God used angels to announce judgment on the two cities, and when they had delivered Lot and his family out of Sodom and Gomorrah, then the cities went up in smoke with all of their people. Sodom and Gomorrah were wicked cities and God was not pleased with them. God is also going to use angels to announce judgment on this world system, as we can read in the book of Revelation. I will try to explain each of their duties later on in this writing.

"Listen to the Angels"

To point out further that angels are not spirits or ghosts flying around out there somewhere, as most people think, I will use the scripture found in Genesis 1:26-27 where God said, "Let us make man in our image, after our likeness --- so God created man in his (own) image (tselem, Hebrew - his and his angel's own figure and shape), in the image of God created he him; male and female created he them".

Here is where we have to explain their make-up to some extent. Some teachers of religion have tried to explain away this verse by implying that this "image or likeness is found chiefly in man's tri-unity and mortal nature". The facts are that the original Hebrew terms define the creation of man to the exact image, figure and shape of God and his angels in every form! For what is intelligent life? Isn't it the very life blood flowing through the flesh, carrying nourishment to the body and brain which results in intelligent life? To accept the theory that God and his angels are invisible spirits or ghosts is to conclude that they have no flesh, no blood, no brain, no intelligence, no life - that in fact they are nothing!

Scientists have long recognized that there can be no intelligent life without flesh, body, blood and brain. A noted physicist and physiologist made this observation on the physical form of God (including the angels, men, and all who are made in their image). He says God is in a form. For every living thing must have a form. Things without form, like dust and ashes, have not life. God has the organs that are in man (like brain, lungs, heart, etc.). Nothing can be alive unless the organs of life are in it. All the organs of man taken together are what makes man a man. God is unborn, perfect man; he has always been alive in the universe. That is why he is called the first and the last, the beginning and the ending, alpha and omega.

Fleshly man is born man, born in God's image and likeness. Born man is imperfect, but the unborn divine man (God) has all the organs of fleshly man in divine perfection. Unless God was a man, he could not have given birth to the universe such as it is.

"Listen to the Angels"

Many Christians think of God as a spirit because he is called a spirit in the Bible, but they do not know that every spirit and angel is a man. While we must think of God as a man, we can't picture in our minds the perfection and boundlessness of God. Canst thou, by searching, find out God? Canst thou find out the almighty unto perfection?

Most medical professionals, from experience with the stark realities of life, would agree with the above scientist, but not many theologians. The myth of strange appearing and disappearing angelic creatures with feathery wings is too deeply rooted in their theology, in spite of the fact that the Hebrew writer states plainly that "some have entertained angels unawares". Angels could hardly have great white wings, as they look and act so much like men that some have entertained them totally unaware that they were angels!

In Hebrews 13:2 it says, "Be not forgetful to entertain strangers; for thereby some have entertained angels unawares" (unaware that they were angels and

"Listen to the Angels"

not men). Here is the biblical description of angels; it gives us the definition and clearest picture of an angel. A stranger who is young, healthy, vigorous, handsome and kind, with none of the mortality marks of sadness, disease, injury, or aging signs could well be either a young man or angel of the Lord!

This is the biblical description of an angel, not the religious one of a flying creature with feathery wings – for it is only with this human resemblance that an angel could be entertained unknowingly, unaware that it was an angel and not a young and healthy man!

There is scriptural evidence that angels are so much like men (particularly young and healthy men) that many have eaten with them, drank with them, and entertained them unaware that there was any difference between them. The scripture says plainly that there is only a "little" difference, that man is only "a little lower than the angels" due to the weakening and aging process of man's mortality.

Even this difference is temporary, until

immortality is freely given to all in the coming kingdom. Since it is only temporary, the weakening and aging effect of man's mortality makes him a little lower, or different, than angels. There will be no difference between men and angels when "the spiritual dead are raised" in the coming thousand year kingdom.

Paul shows, and the mortality of all "shall have put on immortality" (I Corinthians 15:52-54). A young and healthy man could be indistinguishable from an angel - so much so that "some have entertained angels unawares". They were not young men!

In spite of religious theories and myths, the scriptural facts are that God created man in his own image and likeness, and in the same image and likeness of his heavenly host of angels, cherubim and seraphim! "Let us make man in our image, after our likeness" he says to his heavenly host of angels, cherubim and seraphim, and there is not one bit of scriptural evidence that these were flying creatures

"Listen to the Angels"

with great white wings! They are all angelic men, and the names cherubim and seraphim are titles signifying a higher rank or officer among angelic men!

I have written a book explaining that Satan is a man and not a serpent and he is the man with the number 666 that we find written in the book of Revelation. This is where a lot of people are confused and will be deceived by him. I am pointing this out so we can see that God and the angels are also men. God and angels are unborn perfect men and never dying. Here is where a lot of people do not know who or what they are worshipping or praying to.

You can ask people just what are you worshipping, and they will say to you that they are worshipping God. Try to get them to say who or what is God and they are lost for words. What I am trying to bring out here, is that God is a man. No man can live without all of the essential organs that make up a man, except that the organs of God are everlasting and undying. Mortal man is to die before

"Listen to the Angels"

he can become a man of immortality as stated in I Corinthians 15:53. This is just the more reason that we should listen to angels. If we cannot hear them audibly, then there is the written word, the Bible, which tells all about their doings!

God is unborn, perfect man, and he has always been alive in the universe (which is why he is called the first and the last - the beginning and the ending - alpha and omega). Fleshly man is born man - born in God's image and likeness - born man is imperfect. But the unborn divine man, God, has all the organs of fleshly man in divine perfection. Unless God was a man, he could not have given birth to the universe such as it is. Many Christians think of God as a spirit because he is called a spirit in the Bible. But they do not know that every spirit and angel is a man. While we must think of God as a man, we still cannot picture in our minds his perfection.

As I have said before, most Christians worship something or somebody not realizing that if they believe in Jesus Christ, then they are worshipping a man. Jesus himself said "if ye have seen me, ye have seen the Father". We know that according to the scripture that Jesus was born a flesh man and he went to the cross and there he gave up his life-saving blood. I know that things like this will make men's minds turn in circles, trying to figure out if this is true or not. All I can do to help them out, is to direct them to the Bible and try to help them understand what they read.

To point out further what God and the angels think and do, I will use some scripture to try to get a message across to those who care to listen. In Judges 2:1, it states "That an angel of the Lord came up from Gilgal to Bochim, and said, I made you go up out of Egypt, and have brought you unto the land which I swore unto your fathers; and I said I will never break my covenant with you". Verse 4 - "And it came to pass, when the angel of the Lord spake these words to all the children of Israel, that the people listened and lifted up their voice and wept".

I am writing this in a way so you can follow up

"Listen to the Angels"

to get the message of what and to whom the angels are talking to and about. Judges 5:23 - "Curse ye Meroz, said the angel of the Lord, curse ye bitterly the inhabitants thereof; because they came not to the help of the Lord, to the help of the Lord against the mighty". Judges 6:11- "And there came an angel of the Lord, and sat under an oak which was in Ophrah, that pertained unto Joash the Abiezite: and his son Gideon threshed wheat by the winepress, to hide it from the Midianites." Verse 12 - "And the angel of the Lord appeared unto him, and said unto him, The Lord is with thee, thou mighty man of valor". Verse 20 - "And the angel of God said unto him, Take the flesh and the unleavened cakes, and lay them upon this rock, and pour out the broth, and he did so". Verse 21 - "Then the angel of the Lord put forth the end of the staff that was in his hand, and touched flesh and the unleavened cakes; and there rose up a fire out of rock, and consumed the flesh and the unleavened cakes, then the angel of the Lord departed out of his sight". Verse 22 - "And when Gideon perceived that he was an angel, Gideon said, Alas, O Lord God! For because I have seen an angel of the Lord face to face". You will have to read on to get the doings of Gideon.

Judges 13:3 - "And the angel of the Lord appeared unto the woman, (Samson's mother) and said unto her, Behold now, thou art barren and bearest not: but thou shalt conceive and bear a son". Verse 6 - "Then the woman came and told her husband, saying, A man of God came unto me, and his countenance was like that of an angel of God. But I ask not his name whence he was, neither told he me his name". Verse 7 - "But he said unto me, Behold, thou shall conceive and bear a son; and now drink no wine nor strong drink, neither eat any unclean thing: for the child shall be a Nazarite to God from the womb to the day of his death". Verse 8 - "Then Manoah (the husband), entreated the Lord and said, O my Lord, let the man of God (angel) which thou didst send come again unto us, and teach us what we shall do unto the child that shall be born".

"Listen to the Angels"

Verse 9 - "And God hearkened to the voice of Manoah, and the angel of God came again unto the woman as she sat in the field: but Monoah, her husband, was not with her". Verse 13 - "And the angel of the Lord said unto Manoah, Of all that I said unto the woman let her beware". Verse 15 - "And Manoah said unto the angel of the Lord, I pray thee, let us detain thee, until we shall have made ready a kid for thee". Verse 16 - "And the angel said unto Manoah, Though thou detain me, I will not eat of thy bread: and if thou will offer a burnt offering, thou must offer it unto the Lord, for Manoah knew not that he was an angel". Verse 17 - "And Manoah said unto the angel of the Lord, What is thy name, that when thy sayings come to pass we may do thee honor. Verse 18 - "And the angel of the Lord said unto him, Why asketh thou thus after my name, seeing it is secret". Verse 19 - "So Manoah took a kid with a neat offering, and offered it upon a rock unto the Lord: and the angel did wondrously; and Manoah and his wife looked on".

"Listen to the Angels"

Verse 20 - "For it came to pass, when the flame went up toward heaven from off the alter, that the angel ascended in the flame of the alter and Manoah and his wife looked on it, and fell on their faces to the ground". Verse 21 - "But the angel of the Lord did no more appear to Manoah and to his wife. Then Manoah knew that he was an angel of the Lord".

The thirteenth chapter of Judges says so much about angels that I could not pass it over. It shows once again that angels are real and they come to people to proclaim a message from God, and most of the people listen and do as the angels instruct them to do. If they do not listen, then they have to pay the price for their rejection and they could lose their only soul. You can see from the Old and New Testament that this world could be in much worse condition if the prophets and others who were visited by angels had not done as they were instructed.

You may ask the question, "Just how do angels get from heaven to earth to deliver God's messages to the people?". I know that this is a baffling question,

"Listen to the Angels"

but if we care enough about this most often asked question, we can figure it out by realizing that angels can and do transform themselves into human or supernatural beings, as God sees fit to use them that way.

For example, let us look at Judges 13:20 where the angel ascended into heaven in the flame that went up from the alter after he had finished his visit with Manoah and his wife. If the angel had stayed in a natural form and jumped into the flame, then he would have been consumed by the fire. Let us also think of the three Hebrew children who were cast into the fiery furnace by the king. It says that there were four in the furnace and none were harmed. Do you not think that an angel was there?

We can see from the book of Daniel where the mouths of the lions were closed so that no hurt was done to Daniel. There are many places throughout the Bible where angels ascended and descended, so they had to be in another form or dimension, and since angels do not have wings, they have to have

"Listen to the Angels"

some kind of transportation. I do not know just what it is, but if we study the first chapter of Ezekiel, we can get a very good idea of how they move around. Here is a verse in Isaiah 37:36 to show just how powerful angels are and what they can do. Verse 36 says "The angel of the Lord went forth, and smote in the camp of the Assyrians a hundred and fourscore and five thousand: and when morning came, behold they all were dead corpses". This happened because the people would not listen to God and blasphemed his name.

Here is the difference in cursing and blessings when we listen. In Isaiah 63:9, "In all their affliction (he) was afflicted, and the angel of his presence saved them: In his love and in his pity he redeemed them and he bare them, and carried them all the days of old". And he will redeem and carry us in the days of the new, but we have to listen and obey.

In Zachariah 3:1 we find another example of an angel traveling to earth to visit a man. "Joshua, the high priest, was standing before the angel of the Lord

"Listen to the Angels"

and Satan was standing at his right hand to resist him." Verse 2 - "And the Lord said unto Satan, The Lord rebuke thee, O Satan; even the Lord that hath chosen Jerusalem rebuke thee: is this not a branch plucked out of the fire?"(Joshua). Verse 3 - "Now Joshua was clothed with filthy garments, and stood before the angel". Verse 4 - "And he answered and spake unto those that stood before him saying, Take away the filthy garments from him, and unto him he said, Behold, I have caused thine iniquity to pass from thee, and I will clothe thee with change of raiment". We can see in verse 4 where he was clothed in new garments, and in verse 5, that the angel of the Lord stood by.

Verse 6 - "And the angel of the Lord protested unto Joshua (verse 7) saying, Thus saith the Lord of host; If thou will walk in my ways, and if thou will keep my charge, then thou shalt also judge my house, and shalt also keep my courts, and I will give thee places to walk among these that stand by". I wanted you to see that when we make a stand to change our filthy

"Listen to the Angels"

garments and put on new ones for the Lord, that Satan is always there to hinder our change (that is, if we are weak enough to let him). On the other hand, if we rebuke him then we can walk in the ways of the Lord.

I again want to point out that the angel that came to Joshua had a message for him. Joshua listened and became a man that God could use in his plan to redeem his people. We can read on through Zachariah and find where the angels had many encounters with men. Throughout the Old Testament, we can learn a lot about angels coming to the earth and bringing many messages and instructions to the men that would cause many great changes on the earth. We have already witnessed many of these changes. The scripture, along with history, has proven that what these men said and prophesied has come to pass, and is still being fulfilled even today.

These men, by listening to the angels, paved the way for us to walk in God's pathway. All of the

"Listen to the Angels"

verses found in the book of Zachariah pertain to the angels and their visits to men on the earth. I will leave it up to the individual, if they are interested enough, to learn more about angels.

Here is a list of some scripture verses pertaining to angels if the reader wants to learn more about angels: Matthew 1:20, Matthew 1:14, Matthew 2:13, Matthew 2:19, Matthew 28:2, Matthew 28:5, Luke 1:11, Luke 1:13, Luke 1:18, Luke 1:19, Luke 1:26, Luke 1:28, Luke 1:30, Luke 1:34, Luke 1:35, Luke 1:38, Luke 2:9, Luke 2:10, Luke 2:13, Luke 2:21, Luke 22:43, John 5:4, John 12:29, Acts 5:19, Acts 6:15, Acts 7:30, Acts 7:25, Acts 7:38, Acts 8:26, Acts 10:3, Acts 10:7, Acts 10:22, Acts 11:13, Acts 12:7-9, Acts 12:10 and 12:11, also Acts 12:15 and 23:9.

I mention these few verses to get us started in the New Testament. What is said about angels in the New Testament is something that everyone should pay attention to and listen to what is being said. There are many out there that do not care about listening to what God or the angels are saying to them, especially in the book of Revelation. There are many that say you do not have to understand Revelation, including some preachers and teachers. Revelation is the most important book of the Bible in terms of understanding God's overall plan for this world system of things.

You can see from the book of Genesis that God sent two angels to announce the judgment of Sodom and Gomorrah. There we see the consequences of what sin can do for ungodly people. According to Revelation, God is going to send angels to announce judgment on this whole world, and each one of them has a different announcement to make. If we do not listen, then it could make the difference between heaven and hell. Which one would you choose?

I know that you cannot hear angels audibly in their other dimension, but you do have God's word and that is all you need. He sent the message to us so that we could know how to live in this life and the one to come. If you think that there is no life to

"Listen to the Angels"

come, then listen to what was revealed to John while he was a prisoner on the Isle of Patmos.

Revelation 1:1 is "The revelation of Jesus Christ, which God gave unto him to show unto his servants things which must shortly come to pass; and he sent and signified it by his angel unto his servant, John: (verse 2) Who bear record of the word of God, and of the testimony of Jesus Christ, and of all things that he saw". We have to know that John was looking to further things to come. Verse 3 - "Blessed is he that readeth and they that hear the words of this prophecy, and keep those things which are written therein: for the time is at hand". The blessing of verse three has a threefold condition: (1)read the book, (2)hear and understand it, and (3) obey it.

Many will be thrown off track where it says "the time is at hand". It simply means that nothing else has to occur before the tribulation period begins. All of the requirements have been met. Therefore, we must take the time at hand seriously. Before I go any further, I would like to back up to where I was trying to explain what God was like. We will take a look at Revelation 1:12-16 to find out.

Verse 12 - "And I turned to see the voice that spake with me, and being turned, I saw seven golden candlesticks". Verse 13 - "And in the midst of the seven golden candlesticks one like unto the Son of man, clothed with a garment down to the foot, and girt about the paps with a golden girdle." Verse 14 - "His head and his hairs were white like wool, as white as snow; and his eyes were as a flame of fire." Verse 15 - "And his feet like unto fine brass, as if they burned in a furnace; and his voice as the sound of many waters". Verse 16 - "And he had in his right hand seven stars: and out of his mouth went a sharp two-edged sword: and his countenance was as the sun shineth in his strength".

The garment was a judge's robe and his hair symbolizes justice, purity and glory. Fire is also a symbol of judgment. The sword represents God's word. We can see from these verses that God is not some kind of myth, but he is a true and living God,

"Listen to the Angels"

and an undying perfect man. Here is the beginning of John's messages to the angels of the seven churches. The reader can check all of the messages in Revelation, Chapter 2. They must understand that these messages apply to all churches around the world and that is the reason to know them and listen to what is being said.

I will point out that God was pleased with only two of the churches by what they believed and taught. In my opinion, each church should examine their doings. If God was pleased with only two of the seven churches, how many do you think that he would be pleased with today?

Revelation 5:2 - "And I saw a strong angel proclaiming with a loud voice, Who is worthy to open the book, and to loose the seals thereof?" Revelation 5:11 - "And I beheld, and I heard the voice of many angels round about the throne and the beasts and the elders: and the number of them was ten thousand times ten thousand, and thousands of thousands". Revelation 7:1, "And after these things I saw four angels standing on the four corners of the earth, holding the four winds of the earth, that wind should not blow on the earth, nor on the sea, nor on any tree." Revelation 7:2 - "And I saw another angel ascending from the east, having the seal of the living God: and he cried with a loud voice to the four angels, to whom it was given to hurt the earth and the sea". Verse 3 - "Saying, Hurt not the earth, neither the sea, nor the trees, till we have sealed the servants of our God in their foreheads". Here is where we find the sealing of the one hundred and forty-four thousand. These are the ones that have the word of God anchored in their minds so they can defeat Satan on every move, and they know that Satan comes to this earth first in the sixth seal.

The four winds depict God's judgment of the earth, and the four angels are restraining agents who hold back the judgment until God's special servants can be sealed. As I said earlier, God will use his angels to bring judgment to this earth, and here is where it begins. The seven seals have been opened as

"Listen to the Angels"

we find in the sixth chapter of Revelation. The seventh seal contains the seven trumpets beginning in chapter eight of Revelations.

Revelation 8:1 - "And when he had opened the seventh seal, there was silence in heaven about the space of half an hour". The silence indicates the beginning of further judgments. Revelation 8:2 - "And I saw the seven angels which stood before God; and to them were given seven trumpets". Verse 3 - "And another angel came and stood at the alter, having a golden censer; and there was given unto him much incense, that he should offer it with the prayers of all saints upon the golden altar which was before the throne". Verse 4 - "And the smoke of the incense, which came with the prayers of the saints, ascended up before God out of the angel's hand". Verse 5 - "And the angel took the censer, and filled it with fire of the alter, and cast it into the earth: and their voices, and thundering and lightening and an earthquake".

"Listen to the Angels"

The throwing of the censer to the earth represents the coming judgment of the earth. Christ will use angels to administer the trumpets; the blast of each "trumpet" symbolizes the execution of God's judgment. The first trumpet brings fire and hail that causes the destruction of most of the vegetation on earth. Famine and lack of oxygen production will result. Revelation 8:7 – "The first angel sounded and there followed hail and fire mingled with blood, and they cast upon the earth: and the third part of all the trees was burned up, and all the green grass was burned up."

The second trump turns a third of the sea into blood, and a third of the sea creatures and ships are destroyed. This will produce a reduction of evaporation and thus a shortage of rain and fresh water on land. International commerce and distribution of food and resources will be severely hampered.

Revelation 8:8 – "The second angel sounded, and as if it were a great mountain burning with fire

"Listen to the Angels"

was cast into the sea: and a third part of the sea became blood." The third trumpet makes a third of all fresh water bitter, resulting in widespread thirst and death. Revelation 8:10 "The third angel sounded, and fell a great star from heaven, burning as it were a lamp, and it fell upon the third part of the rivers, and upon the fountains of waters."

The third part of the waters became "wormwood", meaning a poison, and when put into drinking water is a sure killer for any who drink it. Many men died because the waters were made bitter with the wormwood. The fourth trumpet takes away a third of the light from the heavens during both day and night. The light arriving from the sun and stars and moon is reduced, leading to fear, lack of crop production and a much lower quality of life. Revelation 8:12 - "The fourth angel sounded, and the third part of the sun was smitten, and the third part of the moon, and the third part of the stars; so as the third part of them was darkened and the day shone not for a third part of it, and the night likewise."

"Listen to the Angels"

The fifth trumpet brings a five-month period of torment on the unbelievers of the earth. Revelation 9:1 - "The fifth angel sounded, "And I saw a star fall from heaven unto the earth: and unto him was given the key to the bottomless pit; (verse 2) and there arose a smoke out of the pit, as the smoke of a great furnace; and the sun and the air were darkened by reason of the smoke of the pit and (verse 3) there came out of the smoke locust upon the earth: and unto them was given power, as the scorpions of the earth have power". Verse 4 - "And it was commanded them that they should not hurt the grass of the earth, neither any green thing, neither any tree; but only those men which have not the seal of God in their foreheads," meaning that they should have the word of God in their minds. Chapter 9 of Revelation describes the first two woes. Trumpets five and six result in the death of a third of the surviving unbelievers on the earth.

The four angels mentioned in Revelation 9:15 are fallen angels or demons who have been temporarily bound by God. They are loosed for the purpose of killing a "third" of the population of the world. They appear to be in charge of the horde of demonic horsemen who will actually accomplish the massacre in Revelation 19:19.

Revelation 9:13-15 "The sixth angel sounded, and I heard a voice from the four horns of the golden alter which is before God, saying to the sixth angel which had the trumpet, Loose the four angels which are bound in the great Euphrates, and the four angels were loosed, which were prepared for an hour, and a day, and a month, and a year, for to slay the third part of men, the spiritual dead."

The sixth trumpet, combined with the fourth seal, reduces the population of the earth to one-half its pre-tribulation level. Revelation 11:15 - "The seventh angel sounded, and there were great voices in heaven saying, The kingdoms of this world are become the kingdoms of our Lord, and of his Christ, and shall reign forever and ever". The seventh trumpet results in the establishment of the millennial

"Listen to the Angels"

kingdom of Christ. Are you listening to what the angels are saying and what their duties are for the future?

Since the pit has been mentioned above and many places in the Bible, it has made us wonder just what kind of place it is. I have searched and searched and finally I found the answer. According to John in Revelation 9:1-12, it is a bottomless pit. I will quote Matthew 25:41 - "Then shall he say also unto them on the left hand, Depart from me, ye cursed, into everlasting fire, prepared for the devil and his angels". John employs the image of the pit seven times in Revelation to describe hell and each time the pit is closely associated with demons; it is also associated with the unsaved. The image of hell may also imply darkness and imprisonment since pits were often used as prisons in ancient cultures.

Obviously, the pit appears to be a place of suffering. If you have trouble believing God could ever make a hell, remember it was prepared for the devil and his angels. Those who go to hell are in essence choosing to spend eternity with Satan rather than with Christ. (First referenced Genesis 2:17; primary reference, Revelation 9:1-12 and Luke 16:23-25.)

Revelation 10:1-11 explains the angel and the little book. Some ask the question, "Did John actually eat the little book?" because they do not know what the little book is. John did not eat the book, but was told to absorb what was in it, and when he did, it became sweet in his mouth but bitter in his belly. The act of eating represents the understanding and appropriation of prophetic revelation. The message is "sweet" because, at last, the kingdom promises are about to be fulfilled. It is bitter because it can only be accomplished through more judgment and tribulation.

Revelation 10:11 is the key to the chronology of the book of Revelation. John is told to prophesy again concerning many peoples, nations, tongues and kings. The seals and trumpet judgments have brought

"Listen to the Angels"

the chronology close to the end of the tribulation period and the return of Christ to the earth.

Now John must prophesy through the period a second time, concentrating this time on the major personages and movements of the tribulation (i.e. - Satan, the beast, the harlot or Babylon system). This duplicated prophecy begins in Chapter 12 and culminates in the vial (bowl) judgments, the destruction of the beast and the return of Christ.

The major concern of the book of Revelation is the judgment of God on the world and the "beginning of the Lord". The various judgments are symbolized in the book by a scroll with the seven "seals", by the blasts from the seven "trumpets", and by the wrath of God poured out from the seven "bowls" or "vials". The wrath of God began with seven seals and will be finished with the seven last plagues, which are the seven vials.

To help you understand the seals, the trumpets and the vials, I will jot them down and it may give you a better understanding of what they mean. The first seal: Conquest (Revelation 6:1-2), the second seal: War (Revelation 6:3-4), the third seal: Inflation and Famine: (Revelation 6:5-6), the fourth seal: Death (Revelation 6:7-8), the fifth seal: Martyrdom (Revelation 6:9-11), the sixth seal: Natural Disasters (Revelation 6:6-12), and the seventh seal: Introduction of the Seven Trumpets.

The first trumpet is on the vegetation of the earth. The second trumpet is on the sea (Rev. 8:8-9). The third trumpet is on the fresh water (Rev. 8:10-11). The fourth trumpet is on light (Rev. 8:12-13). The fifth trumpet is on demons and pain (Rev. 9:1-12). The sixth trumpet is on demons and death (Rev. 9:13-21). The seventh, and last, trumpet will bring rewards to the holy people and destruction of the unholy; the earth will be shaken by a mighty earthquake. The last three trumpets will be especially severe, as announced by the threefold repetition of "woe, woe, woe" (Rev. 8:13). They will be directed toward the inhabitants of the earth, that is, the unbelieving still alive on earth. The three woes are all spelled out for us in Rev. 9:1-21, and it is still the angels that are speaking to us.

Up to this point, I have tried to bring out most of what the angels' duties are when they are loosed to announce judgment on this world. I know it sounds very gross, but it is the word of God. He will do these things, not because he is an unjust God, but to prove that he is God, and that out of love for his people, he has promised to remove all evil from this world before he sets up his millennial kingdom.

Revelation 11:15 explains that the seventh trumpet results in the establishment of the millennial kingdom of Christ. The seven vials or bowls of Revelation 15:1 are probably contained in the judgment of the seventh trumpet. They will occur in a very brief period of time at the end of the great tribulation.

The second coming of Christ, while a great blessing for believers, will be God's most severe judgment of the earth. Since the believers have the seal of God in their minds to defeat Satan when they are tested, their judgment will be rewards for what they have done. The kingdoms of this world will be completely overthrown by the coming kingdom of Christ. Revelation 11:16-19 shows where God is worshipped by the elders because what he promised is now accomplished. Their gratitude is for the establishment of the millennial kingdom.

You may have noticed that I did not mention all of the scripture verses where the angels are used to bring this world system to a close. I did this to try to get people interested in studying Revelation, so they would not be caught standing naked before God with no righteous acts.

Revelation Chapter 19 and 20 bring the climax of the book of Revelation: the return of Christ to establish his millennial kingdom. In both the Old and New Testament, the scriptures teach a literal physical (bodily) and visible return of Christ to this earth to establish his kingdom and rule for a thousand years.

The greatest theme of all Bible prophecy is the second coming of Christ. This was the theme of mankind's first prophecy and of the last message of the Bible. In anticipation of the second coming, Christians should live soberly, righteously and godly. Before the second coming, there are many things that will take place that I have not yet mentioned. These things I speak of should cause anyone to open their eyes and ears to see and hear what is about to happen.

One of these events that will take place is the appearance of the two witnesses (in Rev. 11:1-14) who will return before Christ. God's two witnesses will prophesy, or preach, in Israel for 1,260 days. This will probably occur during the last half of the tribulation period. These "witnesses" will proclaim a message of judgment and the need for repentance. They bear similarities to John the Baptist, and will be the ultimate fulfillment of the promised return of Elijah.

They are also identified as the "two olive trees" and the "two candlesticks". These symbols relate to Zechariah 4:2-6. These two witnesses will be channels of God's power and message to the world during the tribulation period. They will perform miracles similar to those performed by Moses and Elijah (Ex. 7:20, I Kings 17:12, II Kings 1:10-12, Luke 4:25, James 5:17).

These witnesses have power to shut heaven, that is rain not in the days of their prophecy, and they have power over waters to turn these to blood and smite the earth with all plagues as often as they will. When they have finished their testimony, the beast that ascended out of the bottomless pit shall make war against them, and shall overcome them, and kill them. Their dead bodies shall lie in the street three and one-half days, and they shall not be buried. They that dwell upon the earth shall rejoice over them, and make merry, and shall send gifts one to another, because these two prophets tormented them that dwelt on the earth. After 3 and one-half days, the spirit of life from God will enter into them, and they will stand upon their feet, and great fear will fall upon them which will see them.

"Listen to the Angels"

Their miraculous powers are for the purpose of authenticating their divine message (as in the case of Jesus and his apostles). Their message will be twofold: (1) Jesus is the lamb of God (Savior) and (2) Jesus is King (ruler). The miracles show that the King is coming again to set up his kingdom, and therefore the people must repent, or the wrath of God will take vengeance on his enemies.

Another thing that will take place before the coming of Christ is the harvest of the earth with God using his angels to do the harvesting. Revelation 14:14-20 states that, "I looked, and behold a white cloud, and upon the cloud one sat like unto the son of man, having on his head a golden crown and in his hand a sharp sickle. An angel came out of the temple, crying with a loud voice to him that sat upon the cloud, Thrust in thy sickle, and reap: for the time is come for thee to reap; for the harvest of the earth is ripe (the seventh trump) and he that sat on the cloud thrust in his sickle on the earth; and the earth was reaped."

"Listen to the Angels"

"And another angel came out of the temple which is in heaven, he also having a sharp sickle". "And another angel came out from the alter, which had power over fire; and cried with a loud cry to him that had the sharp sickle saying, Thrust in thy sharp sickle, and gather the clusters of the vine of the earth; for her grapes are fully ripe. And the angel thrust in his sickle into the earth, and gathered the vine of the earth, and cast it into the great winepress of the wrath of God. And the winepress was trodden without the city, and blood came out of the winepress, even unto the horse bridles; by the space of a thousand and six hundred furlongs."

For those who read Revelation and this book, and cannot get the meaning of the winepress, here is something that may help. The cloud relates to Christ's second coming. The crown pictures him as the ruler of the earth and the sickle symbolizes judgment as an instrument of the harvest; the time is come to finish the judgment of the earth. The second coming of Christ includes more judgment. To reap and harvest the earth is to judge and punish its people.

Revelation 14:17-20 symbolizes the wrath of God as a great harvest with the treading of the grape clusters in an immense winepress. The cluster of the vine of the earth represents the unbelievers of the earth (those who have followed and worshipped the beast). Her grapes are fully ripe "at the prime" in that the time for God's judgment of the earth is now! The great winepress of the wrath of God pictures the violence and intensity of God's coming judgment on the earth. The city is probably Jerusalem, and if so, the greatest intensity of the judgment may be centered in Palestine.

Perhaps the reference is to the coming battle of Armageddon. The "blood" may be literal human blood resulting from the battle. The amount of "blood" that results from the winepress emphasizes the severity of the judgment. A thousand and six hundred furlongs are approximately 184 miles, the full

"Listen to the Angels"

length of Palestine. The height of the horse bridle is about four feet, the depth of the blood.

When one understands the duties of the angels, as recorded in Revelation, when it is time to reap the earth, it should cause people to listen to what they are saying because it could be the difference between life and death. We can have everlasting life in the new earth where Jesus will be our king to rule with righteousness, and we will be his people. If we choose to follow Satan, then we are choosing death; the second death which is the death of the soul, to be turned into ashes. This is the same death that God has already sentenced on Satan at the end of the thousand years, after he is loosed for a little season.

At present, Satan is the only one with that sentence, but if anyone goes through the thousand years without repentance and change of life, they will get the same sentence as Satan. There is a chance to renew life when the next great event takes place, the return of Elijah. Elijah will be the forerunner of Christ at his second advent as John the Baptist was

"Listen to the Angels"

the forerunner at his first advent. You may ask, "Why is Elijah coming?"

It says in Malachi 4:5-6, "Behold I will send you Elijah the prophet before the coming of the great and dreadful day of the Lord: he shall turn the hearts of the father to the children, and the heart of the children to their father, lest I come and smite the earth with a curse". I do not know how long Elijah will be here, but it will be long enough for all people to turn to the Lord and escape the curse. Another act of Elijah in preceding Christ's second advent is to make ready a people for that great event.

There are many out there today making the same calling as Elijah will make, and I wonder how many people will be made ready for that great day. It seems that so many people are caught up in the things and materialism of this world system, that they give little thought to what the angels, messengers, are telling them and calling them to do. If they don't listen while they have the chance in this lifetime, then they may never be made ready for the return of Christ at his second advent, and may never see the glory of God in the new heaven and new earth.

Turning from what the duties of the angels and Elijah are, I will say this for the redeemed and the made ready people for the new Jerusalem. Revelation 9:21 describes the beauty and glory of the holy city. It is called Christ's bride, a reference that the church is the city's principal inhabitant. It is an expression of the glory of God. The wall described in Revelation 21:12 shows its security and protection. Its gates show accessibility and the gold and precious stones in Revelation 21:19 depict the glory, beauty and eternal quality of the city.

The effect is a magnificent city of brilliant gold adorned with gems of every color. There appears to be only one street also made of pure, radiant gold. There is no temple in the city, since both the Father and the Son will be present in their fullest manifestations. Its light will be provided by the "shekinah", or glory of God and of Christ. The glory of God in the new Jerusalem will light the earth.

"Listen to the Angels"

Perhaps the new Jerusalem will give light to the earth during the millennium as a satellite city. The nations ruled by various kings and levels of earthly authority will honor the heavenly city as the selling place of God. Only redeemed and glorified people will have access to dwell in the new Jerusalem, no sinful thing that defileth will enter God's presence. You can see from this that many out there need to be made ready, and if they do not listen to the angels, they will not be ready. Do you want to miss out on the new and coming city of God?

The only way that you can enter this great city is to turn your back on Satan and repent of all the things we call sin. For those who overcome, here is part of their blessings: Revelation 22:1-2 depicts the abundant life and continuous blessing of the new Jerusalem, where one river, containing water of life (this water being the word of God and coming from God's throne), waters the entire city.

Revelation 22:1 is where he showed a pure river of the water of life, clear as crystal, proceeding out of the throne of God and the Lamb. Verse 2 - "In the midst of it, and on either side of the river, was there the tree of life." The tree of life pictures eternal sustenance and immortality. Both the variety and abundance of fruit are emphasized. The healing of the nations may indicate physical healing during the millennium.

In Ezekiel 47:12, it states that "By the river upon the bank thereof, and this side and on that side, shall grow all trees for meat, whose leaf shall not fade, neither shall the fruit thereof be consumed: it shall bring forth new fruit according to his months, because the waters they issued out of the sanctuary: and the fruit thereof shall be for meat, and the leaf thereof for medicine." I bring up this verse so you can see that the old prophets knew about the millennium period hundreds of years ago. The old prophets also knew what would take place when the new kingdom is set up.

Here again, I'll speak of the blessings that the redeemed people of God can look forward to. Here

"Listen to the Angels"

we can see the eternal blessing of God, and the greatest blessing of eternity is that they shall see his face, though this is impossible for an "unglorified" human being. Exodus 33:20 states that "Thou canst not see my face for there shall no man see me and live" (in this lifetime). Only in Exodus 33:11 do we find that God spoke to Moses face to face. It says that God spake to Moses "face to face, as a man speaketh unto his friend, and he turned again into the camp"

As I have said before, God was a man and this is enough to prove that he is a man (in another dimension). Therefore, we know that we worship an undying man when we worship (for the deeper Bible student). When the kingdom is set up and we can see God face to face, the post-Edenic curse in Genesis 3:14-19 will be gone forever. God's saints will serve him (Genesis 7:15) and will reign with him forever (Daniel 7:18-27, Matthew 5:8 and Hebrews 12:14). They will see him face to face.

"Listen to the Angels"

This will be in the eternal state, the name of God in their foreheads (mind) shows ownership and consecration (cf. 3:12, 13:16, Exodus 28:36-38). Since in the new Jerusalem God is always present, his glory makes all other sources of light unnecessary (cf. 21:23, Isaiah 60:19-20, Zechariah 14:7). Revelation 22:6-7 forms a conclusion or summary of the book of Revelation and they emphasize two themes: (1) the authenticity of the book as a revelation from God, and (2) the imminence of the return of Christ.

These sayings refer to the entire book of Revelation. They are authenticated as genuine by the angel who God sent to give them through John to his servants, that is, the members of the churches (cf. 1:3-11). This is the return of Christ for the church (the redeemed of his people) and this could occur "at any time". The blessings are for those who obey the commands (repentance, faith, perseverance of the book – cf. 1:3).

Revelation 1:1-3, the revelation of Jesus Christ which God gave unto him to show unto his servants things which must shortly come to pass; "And he sent and signified it by his angel unto his servant John: who bare record of the word of God, and of the testimony of Jesus Christ, and all of the things that he saw. Blessed is he that readeth, and they that hear the words of this prophecy, and keep those things which are written therein: for the time is at hand".

I believe by now you can see how the angels did their part in delivering their message to John, the revelator, as well as the rest of the book of Revelation. I did not jot down every verse pertaining to angels because I wanted you, the reader, to search for them. You may notice that I have used some of my own words, but this was to try to make things a bit simpler. Since I have not mentioned the angels of the seven churches in Revelation chapter 1-3, I will try to explain what their message was.

Even though it is recorded in the Bible, I know there will be many that will never read it. The message doesn't only apply to the seven churches mentioned, but to all churches around the world.

"Listen to the Angels"

They should read and listen to the messages recorded in God's word.

The message to the church at Ephesus, "Unto the angel of the church of Ephesus write; these things saith he that holdeth the seven stars in his right hand, who walketh in the midst of the seven golden candlesticks". "The seven stars in his hand represent the angels of the seven churches; the seven candlesticks which thou sawest are the churches" (Rev. 1:20).

Christ says, "I know thy works and thy labor, and thy patience and how thou anst not bear them which are evil: and thou hast tried them which say they are apostles, and are not, and hast found them liars, and hast borne, and hast patience, and for my name's sake hast labored, and hast not fainted; nevertheless, I have somewhat against thee, because thou hast left thy first love".

Can you imagine how many churches of today have left that first love, with very little patience, lots of liars, failure to labor, and have not much love for the evil ones.

"To the angel of the church at Smyrna, say: Write these things saith the First and the Last, which was dead, and is alive. I know thy works, and tribulation, and poverty, (but thou art rich) and I know the blasphemy of them which say they are Jews, and are not, but are the synagogue of Satan. Fear none of those things which thou shall suffer: behold, the devil shall cast some of you into prison, that we may be tried; and ye shall have tribulation ten days: be thou faithful unto death, and I will give thee a crown of life. He that hath an ear, let him hear what the spirit saith unto the churches; he that overcometh shall not be hurt of the second death."

"To the angel of the church in Pergamos write; These things saith he which hath the sharp sword with two edges. I know thy works and where thou dwellest, even where Satan's seat is; and thou holdest fast my name, and hast not denied my faith, even in those days wherein Antipas was my faithful martyr, who was slain among you, where Satan dwelleth. But I have a few things against thee, because thou hast there them that hold the doctrine of Balaam, who taught Balak to cast a stumbling block before the children of Israel, to eat things sacrificed unto idols and to commit fornication."

"So hast thou them also them that hold the doctrine of the Nicocaitans, which I hate". These people were a sect who attempted to use Christian liberty as an excuse for self-indulgence and immorality. The promise to him that overcometh applies to all Christians with genuine faith. To him that overcometh, this will be fulfilled as believers enjoy the blessings of the new Jerusalem, the paradise of God. Jesus goes on to say "Repent; or else I will come unto thee quickly, and will fight against them with the sword of my mouth."

It goes on to say, "He that hath an ear, let him hear what the spirit saith unto the churches, To him that overcometh will I give to eat of the hidden manna, and will give him a white stone, and in the stone a new name written, which no man knoweth saving he that receiveth it." This white stone with its new name symbolizes acceptance and approval by God.

"Unto the angel of the church in Thyatira write, These things sayeth the Son of God, who hath his eyes like a flame of fire, and his feet are like fine brass, I know thy works, and charity, and service, and faith, and thy patience, and thy works; and the last to be more than the first. Notwithstanding, I have a few things against thee because thou sufferest that woman Jezebel which calleth herself a prophetess, to teach and to seduce my servants to commit fornication, and eat things sacrificed unto idols. I gave her space to repent of her fornication: and she repented not, behold I will cast her into a bed, and them that commit adultery with her into great tribulation, except they repent of their deeds; and I will kill her children with death; and all the churches shall know that I am he which searcheth the reins and hearts: and I will give unto everyone of you according to your works" (Revelation 2:23).

Christ is saying to the church that anyone that will not repent for their sins and evil doings will not be allowed to enter God's kingdom. The entire church is urged to repent of the toleration and sins of these false teachers, before Christ has to judge them himself. The church should discipline itself and not tolerate false teaching and immorality within.

In Revelation 2:19-23, you can see that there was a self-proclaimed prophetess at Thyatira whom Christ calls Jezebel. She was leading the church into false doctrine, idolatry and immorality just as the Old Testament Jezebel had done to Israel (cf. I Kings 16, II Kings 2:9). She refused to repent, and therefore would be judged along with her children (or disciples). Revelation 2:24 - "But unto you I say, and unto the rest in Thyatira as many as have not this doctrine, and which have not known the depths of Satan, as they speak: I will put upon you none other burden". Verse 25 - "But that which ye have already hold fast till I come". Verse 26 - "And he that overcometh, and keep my works unto the end, to him I will give power over the nations." Verse 27 – "And he shall rule them with a rod of iron: as the vessels of a potter shall they be broken to slivers: even as I received of my Father". Verse 28 - "And I will give him the morning star". Verse - 29 "He that hath an ear, let him hear what the spirit saith unto the churches".

In Revelation 2:24, there was a godly remnant of believers at Thyatira who had not accepted these "deep teachings" or depths of Satan. The exhortation is to hold fast to what is good and to reject evil. The morning star mentioned above is a reference to the eternal presence of Christ himself. If you want to be in the eternal presence of Christ, then hold fast to that which is good and reject all evil.

Revelation 3:1-6, "Unto the angel of the church in Sardis write; these things saith he that hath the seven spirits of God, and the seven stars; I know thy works, that thou has a name that thou livest and art dead (spiritually dead). Be watchful, and strengthen the things which remain, that are ready to die: for I have not found thy works perfect before God. Remember therefore how thou hast received and heard, and hold fast, and repent. If therefore thou shalt not watch, I will come on thee as a thief, and thou shalt not know what hour I will come upon thee. Thou hast a few names even in Sardis which have not defiled their garments; and they shall walk with me in white: for they are worth. He that overcometh, the same shall be clothed in white raiment; and I will not blot out his name out of the book of life, but I will confess his name before my Father, and before his angels. He that hath an ear, let him hear what the Spirit saith unto the churches".

Revelation 3:7-13 - "To the angel of the church in Philadelphia write; these things saith he that is holy, he that is true, he that hath the key of David, he that openeth, and no man shutteth; and shutteth, and no man openeth. I know thy works: behold I have set before thee an open door, and no man can shut it: for thou hast a little strength, and has kept thy word, and hast not denied my name. Behold, I will make them of the synagogue of Satan, which say they are Jews, and are not, but do lie; I will make them to come and worship before thy feet, and to know that I have loved thee. Because thou hast kept the word of my patience, I will also keep thee from the hour of temptation, which shall come upon all the world, to try them that sell upon the earth. Behold, I come quickly: hold fast which thou hast, that no man take thy crown. Him that overcometh will I make a pillar in the temple of my God, and he shall go no more out: and I will write upon him the name of my God, and the name of the city of my God, which is new Jerusalem, which cometh down out of heaven from by God: and I will write upon him my new name. He that hath an ear, let him hear what the spirit sayeth unto the churches."

Revelation 3:14-22: "And unto the angel of the church of the Laodiceans write; These things saith the Amen, the faithful and true witness, the beginning of the creation of God; I know thy works, that thou are neither hot nor cold, I would thou were hot or cold, so then because thou are lukewarm, and neither hot nor cold, I will spew thee out of my mouth, because thou sayest, I am rich and increased with goods, and have need for nothing; and knowest not that thou art wretched, and miserable, and poor, and blind, and naked. I counsel thee to buy of me gold tried in fire, that thou mayest be rich; and white raiment, that thou mayest be clothed, and that the shame of thy nakedness do not appear; and anoint thine eyes with eye salve, that thou mayest see and as many as I love, I rebuke and chasten: be zealous therefore, and repent. Behold, I stand at the door and knock: if any man hear my voice and open the door, I will come in to him, and will sup with him, and he with me. To him that overcometh, I will grant to sit with me in my throne, even as I also overcame, and am set down with my Father in his throne. He that hath an ear let him hear what the spirit sayeth unto the churches."

"Listen to the Angels"

Laodicea was located about 50 miles southeast of Philadelphia, in the Lycus river valley near Clossae and Hierapolis (cf. Col. 4:13-16). Its name means "people ruling" and represents the unbelieving, materialistic church of all ages. To explain further what Christ is saying to the angel of the church of Laodicea in Revelation 3:15-16, Christ likens the church of Laodicea to lukewarm water, or as being virtually worthless.

Christ says he will "spew them out", or eject them from his company. The hot waters of nearby Hierapolis were known for their medicinal qualities; whereas Colassae was known for its cold, pure qualities. But Laodicea was forced to receive water by aqueduct from other areas. By the time it arrived at Laodicea, it was lukewarm and provoked nausea. The works of the Laodicean church were as worthless as the city's lukewarm water. The description does not refer to a back ridden condition, but rather to their lack of genuine faith.

"Listen to the Angels"

Revelation 3:17-19 says Laodicea was famous for its wealth, its bankers, its medical school, its popular eye salve, and its textile industry. Christ says that spiritually, the people of the church are poor, blind and naked. True wealth is found only in God's grace. The church had no spiritual value (gold), virtue (white raiment), or vision (eye salve). He urges the church to repent of their lack of genuine faith and spiritual understanding.

Revelation 3:20-22 says that in light of the spiritual condition of the Laodiceans described in verse 17-18, the invitation of verse 20 seems to be evangelistically addressed to individual members of an apostate church, so they might receive Christ genuinely as Savior and Lord (cf. John 1:12, 10:27). To sup (dine) means to have fellowship (cf. Luke 22, John 14:23) and to enjoy Christ's blessings. The promise to sit with Christ in his throne refers to the reigning with Christ in his kingdom (cf. Matthew 19:28, Rev 20:4, 22:1) Revelation chapter 3 contains the last reference to the church before Revelation chapter 22.

Revelation 3:17 says "Because thou sayest I am rich and increased with goods, and we have need of nothing; and knowest not that thou are wretched, and miserable, and poor, blind, and naked". I think that we all know what "wretched" and "miserable" means, but being "poor" means we are lacking spiritual growth. Being "blind" we have not opened our spiritual eyes to see and know what the truth of the Bible is all about. Being "naked" means we are not doing any righteous acts that make up the white garments that we will be wearing in God's kingdom.

In verse 18 Jesus says, "I counsel thee to buy of me gold tried in the fire, that thou mayest be rich; and white raiment, that thou mayest be clothed, and that the shame of thy nakedness do not appear; and anoint thine eyes with eye salve, that thou may see". Just open thy spiritual eyes and you are anointed. "To buy of me gold tried in the fire" means to have your whole self refined by sifting out the sludge, just as gold is refined. To be refined you must remove sin and do some righteous acts.

The reason that I have brought out so much about the church of Laodicea is because I think by looking around, we can find a lot of lukewarm churches. Each church should examine itself to see how they compare with Laodicea. I think that any church or individual would be very ashamed to stand before the great white throne judgment naked because of their lack of righteous acts.

Revelation 14:6-13 tells the messages of the angels. Verse 6 says, "And I saw another angel fly in the midst of heaven, having the everlasting gospel to preach unto them that dwell on the earth, and to every nation, kindred, and tongue, and people". Verse 7 says, "With a loud voice, fear God, and give glory to him; for the hour of judgment is come: and worship him that made heaven, and earth, and the seas, and the fountain of waters." Verse 8 says, "And there followed another angel, saying, Babylon is fallen, that great city, because she made all nations drink of the wine of the wrath of her fornication." Verse 9 says, "And the third angel followed them, saying with a loud voice, If any man worship the beast and his image, and receive his mark in his forehead, or in his hand, (verse 10) the same shall drink of the wine of the wrath of God which is poured without mixture into the cup of his indignation; and he shall be tormented in the presence of the holy angels, and in the presence of the Lamb".

If you do not understand what is meant by the "mark on your forehead and hand", it means that you do not have any knowledge of God's word fixed in your head or mind to defeat Satan, and the mark in your hand means that you are doing Satan's work. Verse 11 - "And the smoke of their torment ascendeth up forever and ever: and they have not rest day nor night, who worship the beast and his image and whosoever receiveth the mark of his name." Verse 12 - "Here is the patience of the saints: here are they that keep the commandment of God and the faith of Jesus Christ". Verse 13 - "And I heard a voice from heaven saying unto me, Write, Blessed are the dead which die in the Lord from henceforth: Yea, saith the Spirit, that they may rest from their labors; and their works do follow them".

In conclusion, I must mention Ezekiel 28:12-19. Here we find another group, that their works will surely follow them, still speaking of angels. Verse 12 says - "Son of man, take up a lamentation upon the king of Tyrus, and say unto him, thus saith the Lord God ; Thou sealest up the sum, full of wisdom and perfect in beauty". Verse 13 - "Thou hast been in Eden the garden of God; every precious stone was thy covering". Verse 14 - "Thou art the anointed cherub that covereth; and I have set thee so: thou wast upon the holy mountain of God; thou hast walked up and down in the midst of stones and fire". Verse 15 - "Thou was perfect in thy ways from the day that thou wast created, till iniquity was found in thee". Verse 16 - "By the multitude of thy merchandise they have filled the midst of thee with violence, and thou hast sinned: therefore, I will cast

"Listen to the Angels"

thee as profane out of the mountain of God: and I will destroy thee, O covering cherub, from the midst of the stones of fire". Verse 17 - "Thine heart was lifted up because of thy beauty, thou hast corrupted thy wisdom by reason of thy brightness: I will cast thee to the ground, and I will lay thee before kings, that they may behold thee." Verse 18 - "Thou hast defiled thy sanctuaries by the multitude of thine iniquities, by the iniquity of thy traffick; therefore, I will bring forth a fire from the midst of thee, it shall devour thee, and I will bring thee to ashes upon the earth in the sight of all them that behold thee." Verse 19 - "All they that know thee among the people shall be astonished at thee: thou shalt be a terror, and never shalt thou be anymore."

We can see from the above that Satan was one of God's special angels and his job was to cover the mercy seat. Instead of covering, he wanted the seat for himself. This, along with pride, is what brought his death sentence (at the end of the thousand year reign of Christ). Then he will be turned to ashes to be no more.

Now, to the other angels, Revelation 12:7-9 - "And there was war in heaven: Michael (the angel) and his angels fought against the dragon (Satan), and the dragon fought and his angels (verse 8) and prevailed not, neither was their place found anymore in heaven". Verse 9 - "And the great dragon was cast out, that old serpent, called the devil, and Satan which deceiveth the whole world: he was cast out into the earth and his angels were cast out with him".

Now to Jude, chapter 6 - "And the angels which kept not their first estate, but left their own habitation, he hath reserved in everlasting chains under darkness unto judgment of the great day". II Peter 2:4 - "For if God spared not the angels that sinned but cast them down to hell, and delivered them into chains of darkness, to be reserved unto judgment".

Now may I ask, Are you listening to the angels? Will you listen to them? Are you going to listen to

"Listen to the Angels"

them? Especially to the angels in the book of Revelation, because as stated before, they are going to reap the whole world, and if you are not listening, then you are headed for the wine press. May God bless you and keep you from his wrath to come.

"Listen to the Angels"

Bible References

Ezekiel, Isaiah, Zechariah, Thessalonians, Genesis, Colossians, Exodus, Daniel, Kings, Matthew, Luke, Hebrews, John, Peter, Corinthians, Jude, and Revelation.

About the Author

I am the father of three wonderful children, married to a wonderful wife for 56 years. My wife, children and I have been regular church goers for most our lives.

I have been a Sunday school teacher for many years, a deacon for many and youth pastor. I have been a good husband, a good father, and a good neighbor.

I am saying this that it may help someone out there.

Other Books by John W. Eubank

"Secrets of the Bible: Unlocked"

Printed in the United States
67746LVS00001B/298-339